THE SILVER HOOVES

The second selection of seventeen poems by the finest poetical voice of the post-war generation of English poets.

'You are too good for them Shänne"

Derek Tangye

Further selections of poems by Shänne Sands

- Vol.1   Fidelity Is For Swans
- Vol.3   Moonlight On Words
- Vol.4   Night Song
- Vol.5   Fragments Of Desire

THE SILVER HOOVES

Selected Poems By
SHÄNNE SANDS
Volume 2

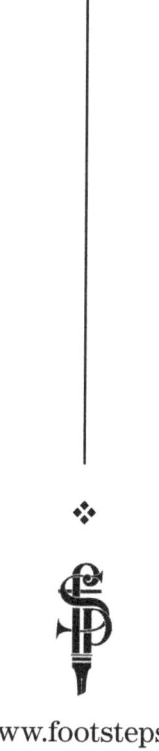

www.footsteps.co

© Shänne Sands 2012

The right of Shänne Sands to be identified as the author of this work and illustrations has been asserted in accordance with sections 77 and 78 of the copyright designs and patents act 1988.

The Silver Hooves

Footsteps Press first edition
www.footsteps.co

Cover design by Kevin Reilly and
Jackie Pascoe

Typeset by Jackie Pascoe

Set in century
ISBN 978-0-9566349-7-9

Reproduction of any or all of this work in any form, electronic or otherwise, is expressly forbidden without the prior contractual agreement of the author. Incidental illustrations are taken from the original hand written volumes by Shänne Sands.

To my son Daniel H

Incidental illustrations from the original hand written scripts

POEMS

The Treadmill	1
Sonnet To My Daughter	5
Whirligig	6
St. Joan	12
Power	13
Mummy How Did God Make Me?	14
You Would Understand Why	15
I Am A Collector Of Useless Things	16
My Soul Goes To Market On Its Own!	18
The City	19
Fidelity Is For Swans	23
Don't Laugh At Pierrot	25
Sheila Fell	27
Sign Here Or Make Your Mark	28
The Flowers of Yammit	29
Sarrat	30
Sea–Theme	32

The Treadmill

They bound my hands
They bound my ankles
They bound my waist
They broke my heart -

Chains made movement impossible
Only my mind could move
Across a land near a world
I was hungry for -

Five voices said
You cannot enter the world -
The world of our fathers
The world of broken statues
The world of pretty gardens
In the rain.

You must wander on the outside
You must bleed from the bone
Outside of green glens
Near full lakes
Outside, outside -
The five-voices muttered
And stuttered then shrieked together
We shall be obeyed -

I was afraid as they held me down -
As the treadmill went 'round
I was afraid -
And my spirit went around
The hard-wood -
The world became a soft vision
Full of tears -
And I became a 'thing'
Trying to undo my chains -

Punishment is a lost day
A weeping from within -
A feeling of ugly, frozen misery -
Uselessness and void -

Then they took my spirit
And tried to make my spirit
Dance to their tune

But my spirit would not dance -
Their music was a death beat
To my ears -
I longed for the flute
The birds' song of love -
I longed for the naked dance of the youth
The swift clear steps of loving -
But the treadmill went 'round
And the ground began to turn to mud.
They found my torment funny -
They longed to see me break -
They wanted my torn mind on a plate
To show their friends -
They sang and ran circles of evil -
Calling to the devil's fairies
To stick black-pins in me -

My spirit did not cry for mercy
The pins did not make me bleed -
I did not bend my knee
To the empire of the dark
I still longed for the flute
For the sounds of loving -
But the world closed about me
And the city took my bound body
And walked it up and down -
Down and up, dirty, dusty streets -

The five voices were angry -
They were losing my broken-dreams -
They wanted me to obey
Instead I prayed -
They had not thought of prayer -
When they left me there
In the dark, dark day of sorrow -

Then the singer came
His voice touched my spirit -
I sang too, soft songs
Of a soul's beginning -
Bondage was not for me -
I broke my chains
And it rained and rained -

Flutes began to play
And colours filled with power
Came out of nowhere
And covered my hands -
Circled my waist -
Touched my ankles -
Glittered from my eyes -
Joy fled through me
Like a purple sunrise -

I was filled with a thousand bubbles
A thousand transparent balls of truth -
Calamity's claim on my soul
Was smashed -

The five voices said -
Turn the treadmill faster, faster -
Hurt and damage
Taunt and torture -
Night and day
Until weariness
Becomes a final agony
And death can strike -

So the treadmill went faster -
And I was hungry for a feast
I had barely experienced
In the world of the living -
But I remembered with a distant
And fond memory -
Like being warm in bed
On a bad winter's night -
I remembered until tiredness
Drew my eye-lids down to sleep -
But death had not yet come -
And my joy-filled spirit sang -
The treadmill slowed to a halt -
I was giddy, but kept my balance -

They undid the chains -
They threw away my bond of hurt -
The tyrants shrieked,
'You are useless to us
We must be obeyed

And you bend your knee elsewhere -'

They threw me into the cold air
I breathed deeply
And walked towards new promise -
The fetters of an ignorant world
Were under my feet -

The voices were distant
And I was no longer afraid.

As I was leaving
They tied another soul
To the treadmill
And I prayed salvation
Would not be delayed
As the treadmill went around
And around the sufferer -
As the ground turned to mud -
And the world did not see
The invisible hands of Tyranny.

Sonnet To My Daughter

My womb once still and silent
Suddenly dilated and gave to birth
A child, my daughter, who went
From me, damp as earth
And small, every limb kicking with life,
In such a moment I did not think
Of her as a new particle of strife,
For the world to perhaps drink
Her up, and in time for her to forget me!
I was content with this moment to remain
A remembered joy and let it be
Always there in my being, where she had lain

    A delicate dimpled girl
    With the opaque beauty of a pearl.

WHIRLIGIG
       (BEFORE AND AFTER INDIA)

Underneath my fingernails -
Covering each dark brown eyelash -
Holding my teeth into my gums -
Across the forehead, where lines begin to live -
Like unsaid thoughts;
Spoken before I realised it
Wails despair from my sleep-filled tongue -
Despair for the veins that
Run with poetry instead of blood -
Instead of my heart the Heath,

Where I can run,
Where running I can fall,
Where falling I can cry
To the ant-infested earth
To mother me-
To take my white skin as a ground-sheet
For my mistakes to lie
In repose against each other -
As playing with fools I found
A shattered glass window
By a flight of green stairs -

The stairs were impossible to climb -
Fragments of thin glass grazed my hands -
Poetry shrieked in protest -
While the stairs creaked,
While the morning hours brought light
To guide my feet,
But nothing to guide my salvation!
Only stairs with open doors
Leading to rooms with sour lime;
Lime prepared for a bitter feast
For the sake of Liberty!

Sheltering under a national flag
Starvation made children's bones
Look like a carved piece of wood
Made to play a tune -
The natives love to dance -
Their bones shall dance to the
Weeping mothers' moans -
Whilst fathers dig graves
For want of better work -

The dead will fertilize the sod
The nation will grow rich -
Rags will mop my sick up as I
Wonder about god in this
Sweltering heat.

Never-the-less I pray -
Having prayed in solitude repeat
The dull sacrifice to all my days -
To look, to listen, to anger at
A statue made of clay instead
Of bronze, which broke as much
As all things break -
Causing the dust to hurt my eyes -
Paying me back for being out
In the wrong weather.

I cling to you existence,
Because a fever blisters my
Hands with heat.
Not caring if I believe or not -
I do not trust the stream that
Looks good enough to drink -
But fetch my water from a well,
Its hard work when a thirst is great,
When a thickened tongue has lost
The power of speech.
This dumb thing can only wait
Believing with no trust
In the journey I'm to take -

To the sub-continent,
Where the open palm will touch
My cheek for gold.
Only annas with be thrown to those
Who beg like circus dogs -
Learning from the pavement's mouth,
Today's food is
Chewed, bought with an anna
That was bent -

Bent as the finger
Which points to routes
I cannot take, because my feet

Hurt me on days it doesn't rain -
So I stay in bed for hours in
A day-dream with my blanket -
Coughing occasionally to break
The monotony of dreams -
Lingering with myself I wonder
Where the rain went.

I remember I was meant to be a traveller,
But views bored me, strange
Customs and the political stench
Of new governments got on my nerves -
Crowds of flesh undernourished,
Idol worshipping and afraid
Caught my attention everyday -
So I swayed mentally half with
Pity, half with disgust, always
With anger for humanity's sake -
Instead of helping I had to run away
To pluck December flowers.

And in the morning fled from
Civilization stinking with
Colour-bar, strip joints and
Betting shops; the gutter press
Fed by debauched journalists
With no hearts, annoyed me at breakfast -
Where oh where did Shelley roam -
Dowson weep, why did my poets
Leap from this human-bridge
Into cruel oblivion?
Fragments of delight remind me
To spin a sentimental record,
But where oh where do kings
Moan their solitude?

Smallpoxed peasants chewed superstition -
Worshipped Krishna on their knees,
Which were thinned and cracked,
Like their backs covered with dirty cotton.
Children hungry, miserable,
Deformed, left to a Hindu idol
By sad mothers who sit
Ringing a handful of golden

Bells - to wake licentious
Gods who always sleep -
Tall, well nourished but lazy
Gods ignore the poor -

In this quiet suburban street
The sweat of an eastern bazaar
Is a memory of coloured bangles,
Silks, black oiled hair and painted sandals -
Nagging beggars invade a super-market
As I buy cheese; within myself I
Carry seas and people, hills of
Tropical flowers, blackened skies
Mounted with stars, a moon I'd
Like to see again -
Great downpours of rain and silly flies,
Strange spicy fish, wet sticky fruits
And peasants scratching lice -

With September apples
And blown fresh earth
My hands rejoice -
Seeds crack open where darkness
Hides their agony as flowers
Give birth to colours and perfumes
Ready for spring - for pretty girls
To arrange in vases -
I shall wait beneath this tree
To fill my skirt with apples, where
Fields like Persian carpets look so beautiful.
Back in my own city nice situations
Block the hours like a canvas ready
For destruction - the abstract
Painting looked finer without the
Oils, the creation vamped the fingers
And the brush; even the feet wanted
To paint or play an instrument,
But gave up this enormous gift for
Dancing the twist like everybody else -

An emotional whirligig drags
Me around a destiny colourless,
Blank and destructive -
Offering a dismal 'thanks' to

Acquaintances met in a jumble-sale
Romance, talking the sunrise out
Of my heart, jumping on a hundred
Toes to cries of glee-toned gossip,
Even national gossip as politicians
Fall only rips my imagination for
A second; music surrounds the
Burial of my favourite voices,
I am alone -

Desire for your body once sped
Me across seas into unknown cities,
My appetite was quietened, your body
Left a vague tissue blowing in the
Winds that rule everything -
I too was blown away - faster than
An eyelash on a lovely cheek is
Brushed with a small hand -
Faster than a sad goodbye, I too
Was blown away -
Correspondence once burnt a
Passionate kiss on the street-door mat,
All that is passed
I am alone -

Again green-stairs glitter
In the wings - I rehearsed my part
And began the climb of people -
Dozens of new faces boring but
Necessary echo'd along the hours,
Bringing an argument, a drink, a
Debt to bulge my briefcase out
Of shape -
Suddenly a lover would hug my form
And kisses float into all the
Atmosphere - dunce that I am -
Took all these mistakes to bed -

Gone all gone -
The peasants, the sun -
Into their own sweet prisons -
I left my footsteps on their
Huge beaches, but sand moves
With the sea leaving patterns

For tiny crabs to scuttle over -
I returned to my own world -
We all do in the end -
No-one mothers the weary tribes
Who lend their hearts
To discovery in overcrowded lands -

Revolutions burst -
People scream their rights -
Night covers every sinner
With drawn curtains -
Auspicious days are named -
Dead men are blamed for past mistakes -
The weaver's task is done -
Children drink free milk and go to school -
Chanting great themes they learn as
Children should -
But soon childhood is mourned -

Tremendous doubts astonish me -
As I trespass my step is my desire -
I want to denounce so much -
Yet useless statements lighten nothing -
For awhile let the birds sing
Above oppressive camps -
Birds sing and fly -
Fly and sing -
Build your nests this spring.

St. Joan

Everything about you shone -
First your eyes with fire -
As voices spoke through your brain -
Your blesséd saints shone around you
Such a glory -

Your sword gleamed and glinted -
Your horse's skin was like a shining mirror;
Where all France could see
The Maid of Domremy
Riding in brilliant armour towards victory -

Your prayers shone, your dark hair - shone -
Your words, your hands, your beads - shone.
Then purity how it was a light
Covering such a proud youthful girl -
They dared call 'a witch'
Whose belief caused men's courage
To seem shoddy -
Everything about you shone -
The ground you walked upon
Reflected your heavenly light -
And then as these old fools lit up the
Faggots 'round the stake
A great flame of eternal light took you away
From your tormentors -
And high above your head -
A halo shone -
Such as men can only dream about!

Power

A sour-air hangs over this tower -
Bitter-herbs are brewed with poison as litter-bins
Hour by hour are filled with the dregs of power.
Stings of hatred burn against the people, winning
Only voices, millions endless millions ever lonely
Voices, in history's pale indifferent winds of no-rejoicing
Only deep black whirlpools suck and spin around a stoney
Joyless humanity trying in desperation to hoist
Their battered souls above their votes, trying to care -
The world's song is a marching-song against the wise -
Bare are the breasts of dying dreams and where
Skies are storm-torn and cruel, men tell lies -

    Beware! Climbing the stairs of this tower -
    The staircase narrows, spirals, suffocates by the hour -

❖

Mummy How Did God Make Me?
(For Daniel my son, aged 6)

God made you out of a puff of air -
Somewhere from heaven near to earth -
Mingled you with all my dreams
Bound with tears left from my youth -
Caressed you with Truth's own breath -
Washed and pure, wisely blessed -
From millions of silver seeds,
Purple gems, strange yet lovely fruits
Fed your ivory-cells with sweets and
Flowers, scents and wines.

He bubbled you to life out of poems
Once divine; filled with prayers all mine -
From laughter, song, dance and golden fields,
Hot spice and tiny birds, then he took your
Soul from His own heart, your blood from rhyme.

Your hands, eyes, mouth, feet, your skin, tongue,
Cheeks, ears, legs, back, spine, guts and voice,
Bones, hair, teeth and lungs from all
My kisses given to your father.
Then God made you mine.

You Would Understand Why

You would understand why -
Why lilac and Chopin go together -
Just before spring or after winter's
Retreat back into the earth -
Our beginning and our end -

You would understand this -
This sudden sadness and lack of will -
When my body feels full-up with stones -
The bricks and mortar of a soul
Heavy with old places and faces
Not to be loved again -

You would understand how -
How to fly across the rain
To a burning sun -
How to laugh wine out of green bottles
And break glasses into thousands
And thousands of happy pieces.

You would understand now -
All you refused to need before -
Before the floors were swept
With new bright brooms and our rooms
Were changed, our furniture sold
And out hearts broken because hearts
Always break -
Now it's almost lilac time
The pubs are closed till 'opening time' -
'Our' books are waiting to be written -
Beneath this smile there's a scar -

You would understand - the importance,
The importance of 'emotional pens'
Lilac and Chopin before love-making
Or after a long journey and sleep -
Quick as a flash a fast car
Passes the window
Quick as a flash time leaves us old -

I Am A Collector Of Useless Things

I am a collector of useless things
Christmas-cracker rings, paper dots -
Coloured string - hidden in drawers -
Behind oak doors - in boxes -
Tucked into books -
Small pieces of treasure -
Gathered together -
Where I always forget
To look -

Empty perfume bottles -
Silk scarves never worn -
Torn little pictures -
My children's first teeth -
Beneath buttons of pearl -
Surrounded by ribbons
Bought for a penny
From a gipsy in Kent, where
We all went one summer
For apples - for flowers -
For hours made of melon-seeds
Left in a vase on top of my brother's
Old dinky-cars -

Victoriana, souvenirs from the past -
Before I was born - green shiny glass
White-pretty china - a fat, ugly cat,
A crinoline-lady - a black-evil bat -
Hundreds of marbles - bundles of fans -
All lacy - all Spanish - all second-hand -
Broken bangles, a brooch of real gold -
A pack of cards with most of them missing
A drawing-pin with a top of brass -
A shell from World War I, also begun
Before I was born -
Left lying near some Gaelic corn -

Dried sticks of spice from miles away -
A basket of sweets - near some bright
Orange straws - notes about butterflies,
Last year's hat - shopping-lists, old bills,
Cotton reels - a skein of pink wool -
Tied around my son's first shoes -
Lipsticks I don't use -

A small stuffed bird - a clockwork mouse,
Left in a corner of my favourite house -
Fragments of chains - a match-box from France
A St. Christopher rusty with age -
Other charms all tangled with hair -
A doll with one arm
Sitting in a miniature chair -
Left by the side of a rusty bird-cage -

Being a collector of useless things -
I also keep weeping-willow leaves -
Feathers from sparrows left in the snow -
Brown-beans that forgot how to grow -
Tomato-plants for some future spring -
A 78" record cracked down the middle -
Also a jug in the shape of a fiddle -
A musical toy made in Japan -
Some Cornish violets - dried in the sun -
A soup-bowl from a special occasion -
One cushion nobody likes -

A few scented joss-sticks -
A candle from Rome - broken earrings
An Indian flute - some of that shiny -
Plastic pretend fruit -
Theatre programmes just had to be there
An underground ticket, letters, brown rice,
Packets of foreign stamps;
Never been opened -
Along with my toothpicks, my brushes,
My combs - in dozens of places -
Drawers, grey suitcases, trunks
From big ships- little zip bags -
Biscuit-tins - my daughter's tatty -
School satchel -

Left alone on a windy March day -
I'll dust them, count them -
Call them quite silly - put them away -
But know with my collection of
Useless things left on a shelf -
I've dusted and collected parts of myself.

My Soul Goes To Market On Its Own!

There's a penny off my sugar
Tuppence off my soap -
Threepence off the tea I try
From the grocer's shop near-by -
But my soul goes to market on its own!

There's a help-your-self basket
And a walk 'round the store
There's a look at gaudy tins of fruit
From apartheid shores!
But my soul goes to market on its own!

From commercial television
There's detergent blue or white -
Holidays for everyone, football pools and beer -
Every type of chocolate,
Danish bacon and 'cheese for Louise' -
But my soul goes to market on its own!

It's a penny off this England
And tuppence off that life -
'Freedom from hunger' -
Oxfam, Billy Graham, Malcom X and Ringo -

But my soul goes to market on its own!

The City

Slowly the city unfolded -
From the folds, a million
Clone-people came upon
The streets
Taking their places
At windy bus stops.
Cancerous bricks, already
Attacked each chained destiny.
Piped music echo'd in their ears.
Frozen tears, like their food,
Remained unshed.
Carrier bags bled from their
Indifference contents of a
Super-store's discharge, were
Remnants, sales clutter and even
More junk food.
Car-engines jarred the nerves -
As impatient feet hit at the
Pavement for revenge.
Sending up to the angels
Mere protest,
From fumed-filled throats.
The middle of the city became a joke -
And the joke a question mark -
Then it began to rain as the
Bus drew up and the clone-people
Vanished into their seats.
For awhile the noisy city
Folded back in retreat.
The pipe music whistled
Along the streets
And the wind howled in jest
Like a wolf who had become
A comedian.
Somewhere above the city -
A civic rooftop held
A hundred pigeons
Sheltering their wings -
The lifts went up and down,
Down and up -
And the cup of the clone-people's
Lives brimmed over and over
With grey-cloned blood.

Permissive dogs fouled
The pavements
Unaware of the fine -
Auld Lang Syne croaked the waves -
Auld Lang Syne -
Suddenly its Christmas time.

From the civic centre's highest floor -
A nineteen year old youth
Unable to grasp the city's quest
Jumped to his death -
The radio news said he died
Then lied about his bones -
He was not yet a clone!
A smile covered the city-face
The same smile each one
And each one the same voice -
And each one the same vote!

The city could never sleep
Always the venom spilled
Across the oblong roads -
Producing huge lakes of poison -
Furtive, wild mice licked
At its edges
And soon learnt how to survive.
Danger and darkness go together
Like hail and thunder,
Ice and cold
Feeble are the thoughts of clones -
Meanwhile it could be spring -
Ten yellow daffodils declares it so -
No sentinels guard this city now -
Only the clone-crowd massed
In and out of shops -
And once again, there is a bus stop -

A fragrance, which could be honey
Touches the air with surprise -
Someone with black, glossy eyes -
Talks of hope on earth for all persons.

But the bee-keeper knows
The sting of bees.

Knows the costs and pains
Of rent and rates and work
And so on and so on.
The deaths at bus-stops,
When its raining -
And the opposed views
Of people we dislike.

The city voices sound alarmed
Instant city is too much to bear,
Alas, a drunken pair
Drink and drive and kill a clone -
Then empty-out his pockets for loose change -
To buy another drink.
At the end of an avenue
There is a queue -
For the asylum in a resting place
For lunatics.
No release -
Only preparation
To be quiet on arrival in Hell.

The roar of the city
Its excellent services -
Its self-confident offerings
Its officials and cunning intellect -
Its patriotic flag blowing -
Its meaningless growl -
All expressed in shop windows
For clones to buy.

A messenger sang in the market-square
This song without rhyme -
Beware of smiling kings and queens -
Beware of false battalions -
Beware of the director -
Beware of stamps and forms
Beware of the frigid city!
The clone-persons did not listen -
They did their shopping
And assuming they were safe -
Vanished into thin air -

At the windy bus-stops

The spirits of salvation
Waited -

A Rock 'n' Roll group
Banged their drums
Clapped their hands
Shouted and stamped their feet
And the city came
Tumbling down.

The spirits of salvation -
Collected the souls
On their lists -
And departed.

Fidelity Is For Swans

Fidelity is for swans -
Man gives a penny-melody of loving -
Constant only to an image
Of eyelash and breast -

Not the best of river-hours
Tucked into small corners
With birds' eggs and wild flowers -

Not for him the long river
The swans harmony lived near
Brown ducks and willow branches -

His tune is the jig -
The fast dance upon flat stomachs -
His eyes roam -
His body belongs everywhere -

In time to his promises
Kisses chime against faces
Leaving a trace of sin
A small disgrace -
A few tears
In the back garden dustbin -

Man keeps nothing sacred
Nothing as white as swan's feathers
He is a bedroom troubadour
His song more constant
Than his love!

He wanders along sex-highways
Until his libido is rushed
Out of him -
By all that's fair-game.

Moonlight by a still tree -
Warmth on a soft bed -
A lie told after-midnight
Fornication to the chirrup
Of a sparrow -

Narrow runs the river -
Two swans male and female

Float upon their love
Till death ends
Their long duet.

Man scoffs at fidelity -
Ridicules his bride -
Throws wedding-rings
To his mistress with
Exaggerated mirth.

So fidelity is for swans -
Is theirs to keep -
Theirs to glide upon -
They know their waters -
Decry the weak -
Their prize is only for the strong -
Their feathers never break -
Their love never speaks -

Don't Laugh At Pierrot

Of course Pierrot still loves her!
Only now the tear is brass,
Solid and bright -
Polished with lemon juice
And kept in a bottom drawer -

She, miles away -
Up a country lane passed the church
And back again -
She weeps crystal pools,
Which along with freaks, monkeys,
Music-collections in damp cottages,
Are seen by 'summer visitors',
£1 per adult, 50p for children,
Who are really grey imps -

Their act black, blue,
Basic situation comedy
Sometimes seen on late T.V.,
When the romantics are kissing
Each other's toes between rows
Of fading Gladioli -
So it must be August -

He has his tearful gloom -
Plastered on cheap lids -
She is an eternal doll,
Stiff and white -
Death in a shroud of Taiwan silk -

My god was this ever love?
Now a seaside card-calendar
Or a rather soppy 'pop' opera
With a bit of ballet thrown in -

Of course it was -
Don't laugh at Pierrot,
He has his brass-tear,
She has become used to crystal pools,
Instead of a looking-glass -
And if they are old -
What a show, night after night,
Forever -

A wonderful act; try to follow it
And you will find egg on your face -
No brass tear for beginners -
Only clown's mask for pretending
To fall in love!

SHEILA FELL

I remember you, Sheila Fell,
I remember your small Belsize Park bedsit;
Stinking of oils -
Your cat's dinner stinking too -
And your black cat as thin as you!

I remember your lover Irish Clifford -
And all of us standing in no.38
Glenlock Road's hall, talking -

I remember lying next to Alan,
As we in silence listened to music
On the 'Third', we artists of youth.

I remember how you couldn't kill
A moth, even if it ate thro' the
Few clothes you had -
And how you wanted my 'gift'
And I 'yours'
You to be poet and I to paint -

Now you are dead; could we
Exchange that gift too - I would
Enter into your enchantment
And you take my poverty -
No stranger to you -

I remember your gazelle-brown eyes
And tonight
At your demise
My hazel-eyes
Weep.

Sheila Fell is dead -
And I, who still survive,
Hear somewhere in my head
The ghost-voices of thirty years ago -
Calling, clear and sweet
As poet to painter
Gives a tear.

(ON HEARING OF THE DEATH OF
CUMBRIAN PAINTER SHEILA FELL.)

Sign Here Or Make Your Mark

The sky is blue its summer-time
Sign here or make your mark.

The sky is grey the following week
Sign here or make your mark.

The benefit book all dates and stamps
The post-office queue all sour and damp
Sign here or make your mark.

Over the road the Co-op waits
To take your benefit for food
The sky above the traffic-fumes
Is poisoned with a deadly glare

Don't moan, don't stare, just wait
Sign here or make your mark.

The shoes are pieces of old scruff -
The sweat-shirt loose and stained -
Benefit day has come once more -
In spite of sun or rain -

Just before you die
A tin like voice will say -
Sign here or make your mark
Then take the book away.

The Flowers Of Yammit

The desert wind
Has a new fragrance -
The perfume of flowers -
The flowers of Yammit -

Yammit was a garden -
And like Eden -
The people were
Ordered to leave.

Flags are not plants -
Peace is of the rose -
Not the gun and boot
Of soldiers' dress.

So the people left -
Their houses, farms
And temple, blown to rubble -

Only the wind -
Perfumed with flowers
Says 'Yammit was here'
Another flag faces the sun -
But Zion has deep footprints

And some plants have roots,
That touch the core of Earth -
Soon there will be no more moving -
Soon peace will be
The desert rose -
For Yammit was a garden.

SARRAT

I was so tired that I slept -
and did not seem to mind
the insects all around us.
The spiders, ants
and creepy-crawlies with no names.
The wasps that were after
sweet syrup from our apples -
The chunks of cheese and
sun-baked, stale bread.

I was so tired -
Was it tiredness that made me sleep -
It was love perhaps -
Then love is a kind of tiredness.
Then waking to find you there -
Smelling of all the wrong,
but so right smells -
That made me love you so.
To find the sun no more
than a tiny speck of surprise in the sky -
No longer a giant of furious fire -
How we loved to wake and
see the small village church
and fading red poppies.
Even the insects seemed our friends
And you were so kind,
When being alive made demands on one.
And then to remember
Miles and miles of fields
All waiting to be slept in.
My relaxed form against yours
Made living so simple -
How we laughed and smiled,
For laughter without smiles is sometimes cruel -
And we did not wish to hurt anyone.
Indeed we were so much with God -
Every pebble on the ground -
Glittered with divine simplicity.
Sarrat and you -
Sarrat and me -
Soon when the day is new again
We will return to Sarrat
And the fading red poppies.

*

You shall always be my lover -
Now has this strange understanding
been released, relived with but a
kiss of long lost remembering.
You shall always be my lover -
The deepest red of a petalled rose
The Chinese yellow of another
You alone can bring these flowers
For you alone
Shall always be my lover -

   (Sarrat is a lovely village about
             thirty miles from London)

Sea–Theme

Awash the rocks with sea–green kelp -
Sea–gulls' beaks yellow with sun
Glitter against sky and cloud.
Wild ferns shake gently to and fro -
High into hills and faraway
Wanders a moorland deep with mystery -
The ocean frames it all, its movements
Captured forever by the watching Moon;
Whose white, long fingers like stems of
Shimmering flowers, touch wave and foam
To vibrate as a salt-filled pulse -
To quicken to life each sand-like seed
And then to free the overflow of
Tiny fish and crabs and watery-spiders,
To speed them all into sea–shells
Made of pearls.
Sea–bright, sea–song, sea–magic -
From day, till night
And thro' the evil storm,
What organisms thrive inside your womb -
From your darkness what births and death -
What monsters and half-grotesques -

Guide me across those pink-topped rocks,
Bathe me with sea–foam, let me glitter as
White-gull near blue fresh air.
Let me imagine sea–gods loving sea–girls
Deep in sand, covered with jewels, unknown
On this desolate land.
Come, take me over waves bound for shore
Far from the roar of tainted cities -
Overwhelm me with sea–might and sea–saints,
Let me feel the passion of huge, endless waves -
And then the relief of sleep near warmed rocks -
I bend myself towards that perfect breeze,
Then on my knees face eternity -

Deep-sea voices call -
The evening star shines above -
Calm small bay, where hidden caves
Keep the voices' echo's clear and loud -
Listen, hear the sea voices singing -
Songs of greeting -
Bright, lovely voices -

Vivacious in their offering -
Flow with sea-words -
Nothing flounders -
All is for the hour -
Special, deep, proud -

Rise with the wave, pale, white Moon -
Transform what was day to night -
Momentary in your perfect timing -
And yet everlasting -
Each sea-bird to its nest -
Each sea-ghost to his haunting -
Each wreath of sea-grown flowers
A garland for the dead -
To tame this ocean in the name of man
Who can? Who can?
There is a trace of footprints in the sand
And beyond the cliffs if you care to stare
Long into space, liquid sea-letters
Will appear written on air -
Read you first sea-poem -
And find the soul's ancestry -
Overflowing on the sea-face smile -
Then quietly walk away,
Leave the sea-theme
To the meeting of those whose kingdom
Is the Moon and night and splendid dreams.

www.ingramcontent.com/pod-product-compliance
Lightning Source LLC
Chambersburg PA
CBHW051720040426
42446CB00008B/977